BETWEEN THE GREEN

Praise for *Between the Green*

"Rich in imagery, bringing past and future into the present moment, *Between the Green* explores the subtle and sublime yearning that lies hidden in every human heart."

—Dwain Briggs, Musician, Performer, Recording Artist

"These Art Ships made of words will carry the reader into the ocean of night. In this ocean, there is dreamlike luminescent foam everywhere. I was tossed into Oceanus' Gut; spit out and slammed on the coral reefs, then gently washed ashore, whole and satisfied."

—Walt Stewart, Certified Leader ManKind Project International, Artist, Singer Songwriter. www.waltstewart.com

"Wow, what a volume of moving material in *Between the Green*. Each piece must be savored and experienced as a balm for what ails the soul. Fox's words are at once a memoir, a philosophical perspective, an exciting piece of theatre, and most importantly, an offering of healing for all of us who wish to live with compassion and enlightenment."

—Bob Beare, Ph.D., Executive Director, The Creative Life Institute, Author of *The Creative Fire: 10 Weeks to Emotional and Creative Fitness*

"Matthew Fox's recent volume of poetry, *Between the Green*, is rich soil planted with seeds that New Warriors will recognize from our cultivation of a conscious life. Present here are love and longing, connection, offering and receiving the gift, deep sorrow and loss... and a healthy dose of the Romantics' passion."

"There are a number of poems in *Between the Green* that brought me to tears. Especially powerful for me were tributes to mentors, friends, lovers, and parents, like *What a Strange Thing to Do, End of Worship, Full Grown Love,* and *The Blessing*. Fox opens his heart to show, in easy prose, how much things change when we allow ourselves, as men, to sink down into the *Spirit Layer* that is beneath rigid judgments and fixed perspectives."

"The poems I enjoyed most in the volume are those that show evolution through a willingness to take apart old stories and use them to enrich the experience of the present moment: self-aware, in reverence, and unfixed. In *The Edge*, Fox states it very simply, *We throw nothing away here, Here on the edge.*"

—Boysen Hodgson, Communications & Marketing Lead,
ManKind Project USA

Between the Green

Wayland Matthew Fox

2016

GOLDEN DRAGONFLY PRESS

For the Soul of this World:

We are all connected
Between the Green

On Bliss by Paul Claudel

There is no one of my brothers [or sisters]... that I can do without... In the heart of the meanest miser, the most squalid prostitute, the most miserable drunkard, there is an immortal soul with holy aspirations, which deprived of daylight, worships in the night. I hear them speaking when I speak and weeping when I go down on my knees. There is no one of them I can do without. Just as there are many stars in the heavens and their power of calculation is beyond my reckoning so also there are many living beings... I need them all in my praise of God. There are many living souls but there is not one of them that I'm not in communion in the sacred apex where we utter together the *Our Father*.

CONTENTS

INTRODUCTION

I do not know what impact my words will have on those that read or hear them. They have been both my solace and my curse over the years. They have come from high places when the spirit rode the currents flying on the illusions of safety and security. And they have come from the depths, when the soul could not or would not turn to face the sunlight of the spirit. They have come from direct experience with the ambiguity of life; temporary pleasures; joys and horrors; unanswered questions, it's refusal to give permanence. They have come from a deep and abiding sense of community and comradery with like-minded travelers. They have been forced to the surface from the pain of betrayal, from the sequestered observatory, from isolation, and even incarceration.

From the beginning, the larger questions have been the driving force, and the poet has evolved and is still evolving. But now the soul is laid bare, her fondest illusions shattered to pieces, then blown across the sands of shifting culture, social and political upheaval, where the lines between right and wrong, good and evil are not so discernible.

These poems are larger in their comfort than in their confrontation. They are my teachers, angels who accompany me, and who will not be quiet. They bring messages of hope or news of approaching danger and the need for defense. The naiveté of youth is both nurtured and destroyed in these lines. I hope the reader finds solace here; a bold declaration of victory against the uncertain night of the soul; a shout of courage in the recognition of our common humanity, a voice of compassion born from a deeper love of life with all of its fleeting goodness, its dangerous beauty and its subjective truth.

I invite the reader to travel with me into these spaces, these memories, these projections, down the middle way; the path of forgiveness; the road of genuine faith that comes only through the crucible of doubt. Join me in a sincere quest, a search for the spirit of place and belonging, between the green.

ACKNOWLEDGEMENTS

*T*here are so many to thank for this milestone in my journey and I cannot possibly name them all. These poems reflect a life going back to the days of childhood and my effort to keep those memories alive. They also reflect a wandering path through many loves, joys, heartaches, successes and failures that have all contributed to the man I am today.

In my poetry, family is a major theme and so I want to thank my mom and dad for loving me, for the values that they tried to instill in me and for never giving up on me when I was at my worst. And thank you Sylvia and Pat, my sister and brother, who I love with all my heart. Thanks to grandparents, aunts, uncles, cousins and all my extended family.

Thank you Danny Hammel and Ann Perkins, friends for over 50 years now. We survived the 60s and we developed lifetime bonds that will never be broken. I hope the loyalty of our friendship you will see in my words. And there are many more friends from childhood who I am now reconnected to thanks to Social Media. I will never forget any of you. I have never stopped loving you.

After getting into recovery from alcoholism in 1985, I was fortunate enough to land a job working for bestselling author John Bradshaw who has recently passed over to the next place. Thank you John for all the love and guidance and support you gave me in healing the wounds of my past and coming to a place where I could discover my highest calling. Thank you to Bill W. and Dr. Bob and all their friends and to my newest friends in that fellowship, Wesley and Sheryl; Richard and Lena.

Thanks to all my life partners for teaching me the lessons of love in adult relationship. Thank you Vivian, my first true love. Though you are gone from this world, I will never forget our young love. Thank you Sandra, my wife of the past 13 years. You are my rock, my stable ground that keeps my spirit from flying into the sun. Thank you to my daughter Cara; you are a beautiful human being who adds so much joy to my life, evidenced by your high moral code, and for two grandkids and one great granddaughter. Thank you, Teresa, for the gift of our sons Ryan and Travis who keep plugging away at the challenge of growing and learning their own lessons in a tough world. My sons, you both have always responded to my effort to love you and prepare you for this life. Thanks for teaching me the lesson of parental letting- go that you might then go and find your own highest calling.

Thank you all who have recognized my gift of trying to earn a poetic life. Thank you Springborn (Red Hawk-Dancer), the first to intro me as poet to his friends. Thank you Sandy Brantley for calling me "Poet". Thank you Rob Two Hawks for your brilliance and for braving the depths of the dark night of the soul, suffering it (still) and then for sharing the wisdom found there. Thank you to Crosby Bean, who has walked through many dark alleys with me and who cries openly with me for reasons neither of us can quite understand. Thank you Stephen Nielsen for always being there for me and for never judging me. Thank you Don and Beverly Burton, your encouragement to me as a writer and your friendship will go with me wherever I go.

The men in my life have been the force behind many of the poems here. Something happened back in the late 80's and early 90's when men all over the planet started waking up. A bunch of us started meeting in an old barn on Buffalo Bayou in Houston in 1990. We were responding to the lead of Robert Bly, Sam Keen and others in trying to rediscover and redefine our masculinity in a face-to-face context to heal ourselves and our planet without war or aggression. That early work led to involvement in the Mankind Project, an international organization that seeks to transform this world from outdated models to sustainable ones. The work is rooted in the upholding of honor through accountability, integrity, love and compassion for all as a way of being and acting in the world. Thank you Walt Stewart. Your teaching and your love are with me always. Thank you Bob Beare for your effort to wake the whole planet up. Thank you Daniel Maldonado, David and Dorothy Williams,

Terry Teaters and all of those early pioneers of this important work .Thank you Dwain Briggs for your beautiful soul and for your efforts to lift the spirit into higher places with your music and your heavenly voice. Thank you Boysen Hodgson for your wonderful pre-pub review and blurb for this manuscript.

This work is a gift from the all to the all. I have learned that we are one family here on the planet and in fact, we are cosmic citizens in an unfathomable universe of truth, beauty and goodness. The essence of this knowledge can be found *Between the Green*. I thank you all.

On Love & Friendship

Then and Now

We knew each other from before time,
As felt thought forms clothed in magic—
Sleeping images in the mind of Mystery

Then and Now.

Becoming as deities of legend
Like the sword maker Wayland
And the triad goddess Brid.

I and Thou, Then and Now!

Descending into the clay feet of humanity—
Taking on the double vision, the dust, the death.

Then and Now, I and Thou!

Heeding the mania of the Soul to separate,
To hide in the wet darkness, to know the self.

Then and Now

Waiting, Expectant, Empty, to be filled by light, by Grace.
Climbing once again, Awake, Ascending to the infinite.

Then and Now!

Alive as before in the mind of God.
Together, all one,
Together alone.
Alone, All-one.

Song for Lynda

INSPIRED BY BRID

Your crown,
  A Golden Storm curling down around your
  Shoulders, Mysterious, Wild and Free—
  Dancing with the wind.

Your eyes,
  Full of the deep blue sky on a cold crisp day—
  Life Giving, Laughing like children at play—
  Sometimes changing into Oceans-deep green
  Far from the safety of land.

Your skin,
  Supple, soft—like the Sand where the Sea meets
  The Shore. Who knows what Treasures lay there—
  Waiting below your Surface.

If I go with you, where will you lead me? To build a fire on the
  Dark side of the Moon—or sailing across waters
    uncharted—or
  Picking wildflowers on your mountain path?

And will you also go with me? To an ancient time—to pay
  Tribute to Kings that no one knows—to help keep the
    animals
  Warm in winter's storm and to watch the first fruit
    grow in spring.

Our love is young and strong and yet as old as the stars—
  We still need the milk of babes—Ah! To sip the wine of
    the Gods.
  Let us go forth with great care, in sweet abandon to the
    mystery
  That we are.

Our Meeting

Two oceans never before charted, collided in the night—in a dream.
They were looking for new land;

A storm arose there and awoke the sleeping gods and the
Inhabitants of oldest earth fled...

Only vessels built by the king's command—with sails made of
    passion
Could venture there.

The gold in me—the gold in you—sunken treasure from the
    shipwrecks
Of former voyages—thrown into the foam of this tempest.

And now the hand of the guest moving in the cloud—calming,
    smoothing
The waters of us until only one sea remains.

The light of day comes—I catch your final thunder yawning—
Waking next to me.

Salt of you—salt of me—tasting,
Breathing the morning.

Between Worlds

Walking with you in twilight—
Between the worlds of day and night;
Between the worlds of land and sea,

When everything is dream, uncertain, waiting for mystery to
    unfold.
And the grey-white Spirit world
Intersects the blue-gold world of salt and thunder.

We ventured out upon the rocks and I held you there,
While you spilled out your ocean of sorrow—
Memories of your own sea going father absent so long.

Then Moon just being born to sail across the night,
Sent the tide in to catch your tears and carry them back
To the place where they began.

We found a castle there upon our leaving—
Empty of its king and queen.
A gift to you in return for your sorrow which you so freely gave.

A Thousand Seasons

I wanted to write a love poem to you...
And I found a thousand seasons of you in a single instant—
Or is it my moods?
I noticed in the way that you are—in waking hours.

With each story told comes the silhouetting of all stories
And I am left rapt in some great confusion.
Who can tell?
The smaller part of me stubbornly clings to my opinion.

We were sitting close, the sun pouring down like honey on us,
And as I read poetry to you,
A tear formed in the corner of your eye—
Or perhaps it was mine?
And your beauty shone like the sea on the night of a full moon
     in that place.

Then, a dark cloud came and hid your love from me
And I was lost and running from your anger.

Retreating into the cave of my silence to lick old wounds,
Or is it my moods?
I watched you from a distance.

It's just the way it changes like a thousand seasons of you in
     one instant,
Like the faraway look you get when you must be on some
     distant mountain

Waiting for me to follow, thoughtful, then returning to attend
     to some task—
Yours or mine?

And both full of uncertainty, waking in the time between day
     and night,
Meet and love in the middle.

A deeper love I choose to give to each of your seasons,
Coming from some soft white place in my heart—
Hidden until our fighting tore down the walls
That protected this deepest part of me.
Or maybe Love has made the choice?
I vow to you that I will not rebuild them.

From the Tree

I know you are watching me from behind your veil—
Your head bent down toward earth,
Beckoning to me and the sword that I carry,
Longing to be pierced and filled with my life.

Stalking you with a magnet heart
According to instructions from before time that were
Burned into body memory with the heat of the first explosion
That brought the dance of opposites.

You in your rainforest
Dripping with juices of forbidden fruits
So sweet to the taste,
Impossible to refuse.

I spy you from the tree at the edge of my desert
Across the gulf of an endless river—
And I long to fall on you hard
To drink in the nectar of your flowering.

We are bound to solve this unsolvable puzzle
Let us build a bridge across the river.

End of Worship

Woman—Oh! Woman
Enthroned in mid-heaven like some ghost-like goddess,
Your chemise flowing to earth—filling the sky,
The dew from your hem touching my eyes.

Subtle—like river power from before time,
Rushing beside the blood in my veins—
Washing the soul upon rocks that do not move,
Scrubbing the marrow of bone against my will—(my wish)

Too long you have ruled my night from deep in waking sleep—
Your angel form hiding upon clouds in flight—
Whispering to me in the darkness
Beckoning to me with your softness.

Oh sister of the soil, womb of man,
Wife of some eternal father.

No longer will I worship you.

Pregnant with grief—I too give birth—
A beast screams in my bowels,
Calling all the forgotten animals to myself.
Woman, you too I call down from your throne.

Walk beside me at dawn and at last light.
Eat of the bread of my body—
And I will drink from the river of you.
And we will know each other as only one knows oneself.

The Cup

And now woman! Do you bring the holy cup that I drank from
      so long ago?
When I first believed?—When I last saw that certain star descend,
Dipping low, touching my youth, leaving me on fire with
      divine thirst—
At once killed, filled to overflowing, yet longing for bread and water.

Do you know that my bones ache from bending backward?
Feeding my body to the wild—searching through long nights,
Seeking the solace of heaven and finding only blue-white stars...
Cold, distant, unconcerned.

And now the flesh of this world is slowing,
Showing the bare bone—illusions gone,
And the spirit bent low to earth remains
Brooding for its sister soul.

I have walked down these streets a long time
Looking for an end to the pavement,
Where the gardens once grew,
And a sweet fragrance filled the air.

And now lady, do you come to me
Bringing your bittersweet comfort?
And the cup you hold—
Is it the one I long for?

Let us find a place, lit only by the light in our eyes.
We will sit together and sip from the cup,
The wine of our life,
The sun will soon be awake.

Still Dancing—Still Traveling

For my friend, David

Dancing and Traveling on the edge—alone,
For so many days or years or eons,
I came across your traveling as you came across mine.
Something in your eye or your story or perhaps 'twas spirit
Kept us circling and dancing round each another.
And too, there were others at the same time, in the same place,
Also dancing, also traveling—we know who they are.

In this timeless place, together since then, still circling, still dancing.
I have fallen apart in your arms while you carried me across
        killing floors—
I have drunk from a cup filled with your tears or, were they mine?
You have shown me my heart when I was blind with shame.
You found only goodness when I was stuck in the blame.
You are a friend found only by those who are blessed—I am one.
Still dancing, still traveling—we know who we are.

Today is the day of your birth–
I am born with you.
Today, because you are here,
The earth sings and we sing with her.
Today, the gods are full of joy,
And we laugh with them.
Still dancing, still traveling—no longer alone.

Laughing

More than prancing and dancing
At the door to your
Enchanted rain forest,
More than charming you to gain entry—
To visit home again,
More than entering and falling
Deep into your warm wet pool,
More than the explosion
Of my life into you,
More than dying into your arms
Finishing me at last,

It's the laughing I like.

Darkness Lost

The sun went down but darkness never came.
All night stores, midnight bankers, and the new street lamps
       outside my window—
All in the name of safety and convenience, have driven the
       night sounds and Shadows Deep into some hidden
       forest that I find only briefly
In the still somewhat private closet of my own fitful sleep.

My ears are filled with clicks and beeps—
And my body is bombarded by the constant onslaught of radio
       waves
And microwaves and technological tidal waves.
And the howl of the coyote is only a memory.

My desire is controlled by the Whore of More—
And I have forgotten what it is that I really want—
And the dreams and nightmares that once instructed me
Now envelop the world and they are broadcast day in and day out
On some twenty-four-hour news channel in a language that I
       do not understand.
And I am lost in some new age digital wishing well—It's three a.m.
And the face on the screen is giving me an 800 number.

The woman I love sits on the side of our neatly made bed—
And she is on some distant shore across a great body of water
That is alive with devouring mothers and absent fathers
Or dead with poison gases—
It is there I will take my chances.

I will swim to her and be eaten alive or lose my breath but
I swear I will not perish. The bone of me will find her again and
We will hold each other above or below the world—the madness.
My voice will keep her sane and her song will sing sweet in
       my ears—

And the dragon will rise up between us in spirit and in flesh—
In passions embrace.

And with all of our love and all of our sorrow,
We will seek out that hidden forest,
Where the night sounds and shadows have gone.
We will revel in that darkness in ritual and in song—
And we will dance ourselves to sleep and fly to worlds
unknown.

And then returning to the morning where our children wait,
We will fill their eyes with what we have seen and what we know,
And their ears with new stories to unfold.
To their hearts we will give our attention and our time.
And we will all bow down and kiss the earth.

Three for Yvonne

Incense

You called today,

> I could smell your sweetness over the telephone—
> Like memory incense
> Burning a hole in the heart of me
> That once held you.

Irises

She painted irises,
Purple-blue-with gold
Flowing through her veins, like
Treasures from some hidden angels' mine.
Leaves of green-blue-aqua swimming
Waters of her soul,
How I long to hide in her flowers
And drown in her rivers.

Foster Child

My woman never knew her father
And her mother gave her up
While she was yet a child.

I held her wound in my heart last night.
I wrapped her tired body   in my arms.
Torn between fear and trust
                                        She wept.

The River

For Sandra

What can be said of my love for you? Tis a river dancing
through me never captured, never dammed. A Gardener has
planted wildflowers, ginger, and sweet smelling herbs along
its banks.

The river has its source in the Ocean that is the Great Mystery
and forever is returning to the place where it began. I am
building a ship upon which we may ride the currents; A sturdy
vessel build by a Kings command of lessons learned, our joys
and griefs, our hopes and dreams, that it might be seaworthy
once we reach the Gulf that crosses over to the Ocean.
I see you standing upon the bow, I upon the bridge; a fragrant
breeze whispers through your silver crown, caressing the folds
in your white linen dress, finding flight up to me, filling my
life with delight.

I am your salty sailor and I've not lost my savor. I will spend
the days seasoning your life, the nights keeping you warm,
new poems upon the pillow. In slow moving waters, I take a
skiff out ahead, you upon the bridge pointing to the shore –
your favorite bloom. I take a double portion; one for the vase,
and the other to sprinkle the petals on the surface of your
evening bath.

Stormy winds and downpours find us anchored, sheltered in
a cove, our senses filled, the earth replenished. And on nights
clear, crescent moon rising, we upon the bridge each a hand
upon the wheel searching starry heavens for the Archer,
Orion, the Crab, the Bull; or some new star being born; a
Michael or a Christ seeking a manger.

I've not journeyed this far til now my love, but the Angel who
comes in waking sleep says: Do not be afraid! Says we will

reach the Gulf soon—as Angels reckon time; says we'll rest awhile, another Captain on the bridge. He knows the way to the Ocean, will steer our ship across the Gulf while we sleep. And when we awaken, new rivers to sail, new oceans to seek, new dreams to unfold! What can I say of my love for you? Tis a river dancing through us!

On Nature & Grief

Earth Grief

Down—Down—Down—Down
Into this earth of me I go!
Searching, searching, searching for something lost,
Something uncertain—
It might be the soul that slays the dragon
And wins the King's approval
And the smile of the fair maiden,
Or perhaps the soul that talks to God in the garden
And listens to Him on the mountain—
And so much more—yet still uncertain.

Feeling so broken without knowing why—
Sadness without tears, grief without name.
Down—down—down—down!
Into this water of me I go.
Letting go of hope, open, willing to be wounded,
Silent—I go.
I have found my path.

Ancient Forest

I am tired of this lonely world of cities;
Of concrete and poison and fences and laws and lies.
Surrounded by all these comforts,
My body has become soft
And my heart has grown hard.
My house is locked against intruders
And I forget to pray for my neighbors.

My soul is grieving,
Longing for that ancient forest
When the skin of me was the skin of the land—
And the bone of me was the bone of the mountain lion—
And the blood of me ran pure—
Like the river blood of the mother—
And the spirit of me was the spirit of the eagle
Flying free in dreamtime.

I Want to Love You
(But I Don't)

Dear Earth Mother:

I want to love you;

                But I don't—
I can tell by the way I don't consider you in everything I do;
I can tell by the way the unconscious garbage of my life
Sits on the curb—while my trash container sits waiting
With its mouth open.

I don't love you because the air conditioner says I don't have
to;
I don't love you because telephones and automobiles and
computers
And late night TV all say I don't have to.

I don't love you because those who could teach me how to love
you
Have been locked away—fenced off like cattle to the
slaughter—
Given poison and TV sets of their own.

I want to love you but I don't know how.
Please forgive me for my ignorance.
Please have mercy on the children—
When you raise up to clean your house!
I want to love you—

                But I don't.

Revelation

The grass cutters came today,
Looking like a vision from the Book of Revelations!
Fire spitting creatures descending on the grasses,
Cutting, chewing, and eating the quiet.
These grasses packed tight in plastic, then stacked neatly
Along the curb waiting for second death.
In some landfill they will fall—
Some Hades already full of the shit of people's lives.

The tear that rolls from the corner of my eye
To the corner of my mouth—
Tastes just like the ocean.
Looking up, I see the tops of trees—
Swaying, gently reaching,
Breathing the breath of some unseen life giver.

The grass cutters are in me—cutting, chewing;
I am in the grasses waiting for death;
The ocean is in me rolling, tasting;
I am in the tree-tops swaying, reaching, and breathing;
I am in the life giver.
The life giver is in me.

Fire of Life

What is this restlessness in these men?
Something deep inside aching to begin—
To be expressed in outer form
All the fury of the storm—
Not to hurt or maim or kill,
But just to feel the power fill
The heart with fire of life again.

Ah! But the way goes through the pain:
Through the grief of all those slain,
In all the unholy wars we've fought—
Have all these deaths been for naught?
And what of the red man and his plight?
Have we forgotten about his right?
His blood screams out from the dust—
The earth remembers the broken trust.
Is there nothing we can do
To mend this way, start anew?

The way leads to the tears,
Through the unsaid sadness of the years—
And this is the journey we must make,
This is the risk we must take—
It's the restlessness that's in these men,
Grief inside aching to begin—
To be expressed in outer form,
All the fury of the storm—
Not to hurt or maim or kill,
But just to feel the power fill
The heart with fire of life again.

Searching for the Ocean

The river runs on—sometimes finding wide, slow places—
Calm on the surface—quiet mornings at home
With the lady of a thousand smiles.

Then turning, erupting into a narrow, violent,
Rock laden stretch—the river runs on.
She says she has to leave now—taking her
Sweet smell, velvet skin and her color,
Says I don't respect her.

The river, now red with the blood of ancient wounds,
Taking me down these mountains of bliss—
Through the valley of tears—
Searching for the ocean.

Tribute to Springborn
"Red Hawk Dancer"

What a Strange Thing to do

Who was he?

I knew him as a man dancing the red road.
He came to intersect this world, to contradict its ways,
To live by faith.—What a strange thing to do.

I remember his hands most of all—almost soft,
Mother like, giving birth to the places where they touched.
I wonder if his paintings know that he is gone.

I remember his lips on my cheek—he always brought
The kiss that traveled a path to the heart, warming it,
Waking it gently.

He was always making giveaway: some rock that he had
Found in a distant place and then spent all day rubbing,
Smoothing, using only the oil from his skin;
Or a lock of hair from the tail of a white wolf;
Or a feather from a hawk or a turkey.

Did he gift you a gift also? Do you remember?
Some reminder of a circle where you sat with him—
Sacred in its birth—or yours. Did he calmly, forcefully
Call you to be still enough, long enough to hear a holy sound?

Where is he now, this mystery of a life?
Who among us understood him, or walked with him down some
Forest trail to pray?

What I know for sure is that he is gone! Free from this world that
We know. And you and I are still here with a grief and a groan—
These jagged questions tearing at the innermost places to make

More room to hold the joy of this life.
And I am more than I was before knowing him, this man
        who came
Dancing the red road, intersecting this world, contradicting
its ways,
Living by faith.

What a strange thing to do!

Frozen Ponds

November gray came like a thief,
Or some God Fucker,
Stealing her colors—her flavors
Of reds-oranges like sunrises,
Living green and blue touching
Velvet like irises that she painted
Deep aqua-blue oceans breathing
And yellow shining faces—childlike
Woman—sighs in morning softness
Of fleshy breasts—naked standing
To the gentle touch of me.

She's gone now and everywhere
Is winter's north.
I walk alone on frozen ponds
Looking for a soft spot
To fall in and lose my breath
To the cold.

Blue Ridge Fall

The world, my world, seen through eyes half open, opening
Toward closing, weeping, falling apart on October's mountain—
Seeking renewal of the long sleep—like always.

As maple and poplar, elm and oak bleeding together downward
Upon elderberry, goldenrod and bittersweet, painting the earth
With blue red grief's, memories orange and yellow gold, forgetting
Who they are, finally brown and black, sleeping.
This most glorious offering.

Eros too, seems to die—the boy-man-god knowing the reason
      behind seasons

Leaves us for a time, maybe leaves time behind.

He will grow a beard and travel incognito, or

Become a bear in winters cave, or perhaps an old sage full of
      stories and wine

Warming himself in some tavern—keeping Desire alive.

And what of me? I wait here—still erect—but uncertain,
      wavering in middle years,

Longing for the winding road to call again, listening for the
      voice of wonder—

A child who also waits beside the throne, evergreen.
      Asheville, NC

On Poetry

Unfinished

Unfinished,
My poems scream at my silence
From some lofty mountaintop—
The words falling on me.

Heavy in the sun's full light or rising up from below,
From some wet dark hole where they haunt me from shadow.
These needy children, half born, demand my attention—
Longing for full measure—to become gods of the morning
        bringing hope—
Or demons of midnight tearing down all that is built.

And I am here in service to young ones with mouths open,
And to woman who at once comforts and kills.
Days spent seeking the medium of exchange—
At least a month's supply—instead of my daily bread.
And my poems scream at me constantly.

I want to quit the world! Climb the mountain and fill the
        empty page.
Or descend into the pit and worship in the dark. But,
The terrible onslaught of the clock's ticking dashes my hope
And I am reminded of who I now serve.
And my poems scream at me constantly.

Let it be so for now.
The mountain will be waiting,
The marshland grows rich with darkness,
And on some morrow I will travel the path where the words
Will all find places on another page.

To be a Poet

How ludicrous—impossible!
  What divine madness!
    Such wonder!
      Such sweetness!

You want to be a poet?—Listen to this:

A poet is a sculptor of liquid language;
  Witness of spirit made flesh;
    Keeper of experience of feeling—held still for
    an instant,
      Then turned to blood.

To be a poet, make a friend of darkness,
Let the sun catch fire.
Ah! But you sit at your daily tasks
Assigned by the voices of mothers and fathers
and lovers of systems.

You must quit your squalid hut—this temporary footed shelter.

Rise up and become the Voices Ear,
  The Dancers Dance.
Throw off the chain of circumstance:
Step into the shadow of night, into the certainty of illusion,
The wisdom of uncertainty.

The sun dawns in the darkness—
Untold treasures just for the speaking.

Words 1.
(Yogic Exercise)

Footed	Fantasy
Present	Tense
Power	Emerge
Heart	Barrier
Lesson	Veil

The inner tension between spirit and flesh marks the barrier.
In the present fantasy, I am footed.
The heart—a veil to the emergence of power,
Remains the only lesson.

Words 2.
(Yogic Recipe)

Egg	Flower
Season	Reason
Belief	Falter
Morrow	Serpent
Tower	Salt
Taste	Traveler
Pure	Faith

When the cracking of egg
Signals the rising of flower,
A season of reason passes away
And all belief falters.

Ah! But morrow will come—
And travelers, weary of tasteless salt
Will finally mount the serpent
And ascend the tower of pure faith.

Soul of a Poet

Soul of a poet;

          Busting out of the trap—

Of all past learning,

          Yearning for the present—Now!

A gift to begin

          Burning bridges to all that he knows.

Nose turned skyward, hoping, ascending,

Crashing into self—

Turning, downward spiraling, downward—

Sweet grief calling him to his mourning.

Morning comes—

          His wage is earning—

The soul of a poet.

The Key

The only reason I have for writing these poems is because if I don't
the earth will die!

There is an animal inside—He is hungry for the food of freedom.

But he sits alone inside his culture cage—waiting for you
to bring the key.

He wants to turn off all the street lights at day's end and shut
down the roaring city motor.

He wants to dance in silhouette with angels and demons down
dark alleyways with a vision of love.

He wants to find you again by the light of the stars and fall
down naked in grassy-green fields far from the prison
of respectable people.

He wants to enter your soft, hot spring and be finished forever.

He wants to eat of the free fruit of garden gone wild.

He wants to grunt and piss on the earth.

He wants to be real.

He wants to smile and grow hair washed by the rain and
combed by the wind.

He wants to be certain of nothing and unafraid of everything.

He wants to live out in the open.

He wants to tear down fences and rip up the concrete.

He wants to go home to a place in cellular memory—to Eden.

He wants to forget himself and REMEMBER who he is!

Of Spirit

In the Winking of God's Eye

In the winking of God's eye,

We leave our home and come here
                To wander

Like Bedouins across the Desert of our Longing,
                Or to sail

Like mariners across the Ocean of our Thirst.
                The nowhere

Of our former home,

Almost forgotten,

Like shadows we no longer notice,
                Calls to us

In our dreams, in meetings with kindred spirits;
                In the eye

Of the stranger bent down on the street,
                In every holy word spoken,

Waking us from our sleeping—

All in the winking of God's eye.

Surrender

Oh, sweet, sweet, sweet surrender;
Like leaves in gold and glimmering in sunlight in twilight—
Falling in autumn wherever the wind
Whispers you to sleep in the bosom of mother.

Oh, sweet, sweet, surrender;
Why do you elude me?—Well within my reach yet,
So beyond my grasp—You beckon me and I do not answer thee,
Though it is my greatest desire.

This internal battle—age old—will not cease and I find no
       place to rest—
For the mouthy voice of I—trumpeting its petty grievances—
Endlessly defending its status quo, will not abide in silence,
Sweet, sweet, sweet, silence.

Silence such that the gentle voice of eternity can bestow its
       gift of peace,
And I am weary, so weary of this ancient war.
Nevertheless, I will fix my gaze upon hope and I will continue
       the journey
As long as there is breath.

Second Coming

Jesus came back just like we were told!
But he did not stay long, so the story goes.

There were no crowds cheering, no bugles, no crown.
No holy water to sprinkle the ground.

No churches were open to stranger or friend,
While ministers on high ran for election.

Now Jesus was so shocked—he became deathly ill.
With fever so high, he just forgot his father's will.

I was told by the doctor that he'd gotten much worse
He was gone back to heaven taking with him our curse.

Now—I heard through the grapevine that all the gods got sick.
And to save them from death, we had better act quick...

Well! I think one good turn deserves another—
To settle the score, a sacrifice we will offer.

Oh! But who, who, who will volunteer?

Is it really true that Love conquers fear?

Remember

Let us lie down and die in the empty spaces—
Between the petals of the rose,
Where only angels flying from the tongues of poets
Survive the relentless onslaught of time.

And there in the timeless dust of night,
Forgetting that we are fallen,
And called from the light of a distant star;

We will rise on the smoke of our burning memories—
To the house beyond human gods and cause,
Where the old ones are free;

And there remember, remember, remember

Spirit of Place

When the rose loosened its petals,
They fell upward and became perfume for the old ones.
And seeing a miracle, I closed my eyes
And the fragrance ignored me (ascending).

Ears became deaf to the sound of riot,
As all the rules were being broken.
And touching the wind of that storm,
I ran and hid myself from true power.

My taste exceeding my thirst left me wanting
As I refused to drink from these ancient waters.
And I stayed there in that terrible uncertainty
Until the crack appeared—And the light came in.

And with eyes aflame, seeing beyond blueprint,
Mixing in voices ear, the always song singing,
Touching body majestic, tasting the scent feeding
All of earth and sky and sea knowing the spirit of place

A Prayer

In the first morning light,
When the dreams and nightmares of darkness fall westward—
Let me awaken to the possibilities of the rising sun.
All is Hope, Breath, Being Born
As each life form lifts the spirit from the slumber of the soul.
Let there be a quiet time,
Absent of busyness and striving—
To meet the day in prayer.
Only then may I go forth empty of petty grievances.
Let me hold my tongue when tempted to speak
That I might converse in the chamber of my heart
And there discover a higher good.
Help me to remain anonymous in kindness and gifting,
Just as the invisible breath fills my lungs without notice.
Let me love gently and certainly.
And when I empty my voice,
Let it be for the speaking of truth or to impart a kind word.
Let me become a humble servant
That I might be the master of my life.
Christmas 2000

Between the Green

The stranger picking rags on the street—
Sores screaming on his half nude body,
The lady at her door, thighs used up,
The comfort that she brings, denied to her.
The priest worshipping in his hand-me-down prison
Behind worn out whitewashed walls of doctrine.

I pray for a miracle, the end of this suffering:
Let us return to Eden and earth
Awake.

In the garden, in the soft gray-white light of morning,
I lean down, down, down, below the roar of the city motor—
I see the forgotten paradise there, between the green,

And with memory awakened in each life form,
I circle and gently touch the love that waits there
For the stranger, the lady, and the priest.

Spirit Layer

A greater,
Immeasurable,
Wonderful,
Flowing Happening
On the spirit layer—
Between earth and sky,
Between ocean and wet,
Between fire and burning,
Between breath and breathing,
Where the forever illusive present—
Always unliving and undying
Sings a silent song.

Awakened

Living out this ancient dream
Outside—on the wings of illusion,
I slowly awaken and must come dancing with the opposites,
In the chamber of my heart—where paradox is law—
And weakness becomes strength as all things that I value are
       laid to waste.

Helplessly balanced on a razors edge,
The sword of truth is given,
Cutting deep into the night—painful, awful, and—joyful—the light.

What kind of madness is this?
To walk this path of faith,
Where sorrow is my constant friend?

Yet when I drink deeply from this cup,
My sorrow becomes a brief glimpse of the eternal—
And I am filled with hope.

The Edge

I went down to the edge of the village where the scarred ones go.
To a Holy place where wounded priests meet.

They come to seek out the depths,
To
Taste life and—
To
Flirt with death.

They come after the day and before the night,
In a time when madness rules.

I find passion when the demons and angels draw near.
Life and death merge into one and light and darkness have
        no home.

Here on the edge a meal is served.—
We feast on memories and drink from each other's tears.

A sacred trust is born here,
Nurtured by a bittersweet mixture of safety and danger.
Here, I make friends with my fear, dismiss my guardians' front
        to rear
And let love pierce my heart.

Here on the edge, rage finds a place to rest.
Anger is blessed and sorrow has honor.
We throw nothing away here,
Here on the edge.

On the Family

Full Grown Love

He walked in standing tall, a little bent but not broken,

Spitting out complaints or compliments from his mostly
toothless mouth.

After her death, all of his fears came like zombies by twos and threes

Out of some dark cave within caves where they had been kept
locked away.

After 48 years of learning to be with Ruthie Mae (he called
her Dutch),

At 74 he's gone to war, drafted against his will to fight a battle
with himself.

The doctors have found the rust in him too.

Maybe an empathic suffering for his atonement with
mother—who knows?

I search for a place to fill up with this scream that's stuck in
my throat—

Holding back the ocean, the sad ocean.

Now he is laying flat, tubes spaghetti-like around his head and
on his chest

Going everywhere and nowhere—out of his birdlike mouth
and his giant nose.

Three openings in as many weeks—maybe he wants to go
with Dutch.

In recent years, they were always together.

First the lung, the small alien living there, they cut it out along
with its house and part of the neighborhood too. They had
to make sure they got it all. Then a week later, the colon, Oh!
God! Not that—Now it's half gone too. I wonder what they did

with the rusted flesh. Maybe mother knows—she always knew where to look.

Another week then came the leak around the stitches in the colon. Now he is helplessly open, his inner workings lying beside him on the bed attached to a plastic bag. He's laid there for weeks now unable to talk, sometimes the whisper on his lips, no longer the complaint or compliment, no longer walking tall, he points with his finger to God knows what.

His only arm is tied to the bed (his other arm lost in another war) to keep him from pulling out the tubes that keep him breathing and draining. I hold his head and caress his face. I see the child living there within the full bodied man—the softness, the brokenness. Maybe he wants to go with Ruthie Mae. I almost wish he could or would.

I want to stop this, this falling apart. I want to kiss his cheek with eyes open—his and mine, hug away all the tension from the early years that still at times hovers between us like a dark cloud that blocks out the sun. I want to rebuild with him, be the son that he desired, carry on the business, tend the garden that we built for mother, but she's gone.

And he is hanging on by a golden thread, his appetite, his will, or some other force. There are knots in this thread—knots for each victory of his life. These victories seem empty now— the knots containing strength are loosening, unraveling, becoming the slow surrender, but he has another victory now. My victory too.

He has won the full grown love of his son.

Grandfather

White headed from birth—they called you "Fuzz,"
With thumbs big as a fist and a grip like a vice—
From the daily milking I was told

A man of the soil, struggling without complaint through your life
Which you chiseled out of the bounty of earth.
Ten children, one of them my own dear mother—
I wish I had known you then.

I knew you in the later years when you had to leave the land
Go to work in some building—to learn the way of PROGRESS!
I know the land missed your attention when you left each
        morning.

I miss the callused but kind way that you were—
Always opening your home to stranger or friend in need
Sharing your hearth, your quiet strength.
I wonder if you knew then or even now how connected you
        were to life.

I remember how Granny used to scold you on those hot
        summer evenings
How you would pull off your boots and dump the dust of the
        day in the middle
Of the front room floor—you just smiled, maybe winked at me,
Ignoring her—without absence or regret.

And those Saturday nights in summer's lazy days
When the relatives and neighbors would gather in that too
        small front room
To make music with their banjos and fiddles and that ole piano.

You would make home-made vanilla ice cream—
in a hand crank maker—sometimes it was peach.

And my brother, sister, and me and all those cousins (there must have been a hundred of us) running wild in the front yard and out in the barn and in the field beside the house— barefoot and happy.

When the navy base job ended, you returned to wandering
        your land again.
Completely content to tinker in your junk—your treasure.
From sunup to sundown you roamed that old homestead
Returning to the house only to fill the coffee cup.

When visitors came, your countenance would light up as the day would be spent in good conversation that you loved so much. You would follow them out to their car and talk another half-hour before they could get away.

The night you left us for good:
You simply closed your eyes at the end of a day well spent
        never to awaken—
No warning, no sickness—Almost like you just decided to
        leave in a dream and not come back.

I did not attend your being laid down.
I don't know why.
I miss you granddad.

Mother

Barefoot, brown-skinned, big eyed, hands and feet soiled with the love of earth. Running through open fields among buttercups, cockleburs, and other wild things.—The cut on my foot forces me to turn homeward, to safety. You hear my cry and come running as if it were your wound. The tears of those years, you dried again and again with your love and warmth and shelter.

Then suddenly, almost overnight, sixteen arrives and once again I turn towards home. I am not so quick to show you my wound—my first heartbreak. You understand and try to mend it.—You know your effort is futile.—You try anyway, as if it were your heart.

In my twenties—now you spend your nights worrying as I chase illusive dreams all over the country. You visit me in jails and hospitals—you wonder if I am eating, if I am all right. The door to your house is always open for me to return to lick my wounds like a young warrior who has lost the battle of trying to become a man. I lie to you—say I'm gonna get straight—I really want to—you hope it's true—you never lose hope. I feel your pain as if it were my pain.

In my thirties—more settled now—but still very wild and not yet a grown man. I call on you for help—Mom, the kids need shoes—I ran a little short this week —can you send me fifty. You always pick up the pieces—pay the price as if they were your debts.

In my forties now with my own barefoot, brown skinned, big eyed boys—I spend time reflecting on my relationship with you. I am filled with awe at this life we call mother. I see you often in the way I clean the kitchen, or make the boys bathe or worry about the bills.

As of late, my eyes and ears and thoughts have turned towards father and I know you can sense it. I have finally become a man. Even so, there is a part of me that remains a child... connected to mother.

On my Father's Visit

At seventy-two, when you speak, your words are like
Bright lights chasing shadows into corners where you say they
      belong.

I fought your speaking most of my life,
Tried to ignore my darkness—defending my complaining.

I will remember the words you spoke on your recent visit:
"Bless every day" you said,

"The bones of man hasten to the clay;
Whether it be pain or gay,
Bless every day."

The Leaving

When did it happen?—Your growing I mean—
Wasn't it just a short time past—I was holding your small body,
Your bones still soft—your eyes too big for your head
Gazing up at this giant, this god?
We compared hands and feet—
And we laughed from our bellies.

Sometimes you cried out in the night—I came—
Or you slid in next to me unnoticed to spin your dreams in safety.
Later—perhaps the next day, we doctored cuts and bruises—
We laughed, we fought, we cried.

This morning I was watching as you put on your size 10 sneakers.
At twelve, your body, birdlike, stretching, to peer out of your nest—
Getting ready to fly.
You refused the hug I offered, I wanted.

Your friends will soon be calling—
The night awaits your wandering—
I will fight your leaving.
I will lose.

The Ancient Order

At seventeen, the son wears the mask of the stranger—
One decorated with instructions from an ancient order.
Some of my friends say: "Put big chains on him like you would
     a baby elephant!"
Some others say: "Let him go free or he will destroy your house."

At forty-six, the father, eyes and heart open, bends again
     toward earth
To plant seeds of spring, with instructions from an ancient order,
The stranger has left the house and travels to a land of shadow
Seeking his own calling in the time between day and night.
The ancient order kept, the son wanders, the father grieves,
     and the spring comes.

Seeds have been planted before, given by the father's own hand.
Some under fair March skies when the son was born
And the promise of new life was in both hearts—
Some in the barefoot days of summer
When the promise of abundance was in both hearts—
Some with the falling of leaves to blanket the earth
And the promise of daydreams was in both hearts—
Some with December's darkness when earth turns within
And the promise of slumber was in both hearts.

The grandfather knows the son, the stranger, and the father—
In his bending, he has touched the earth enough to remember
     who he is.
At seventy-five, he gives the blessing and the warning to the
     stranger and the
     father.
In the middle place where I stand, the heart breaks open like
     the cracking of an egg,
The stranger, now with wings from the ancient order, seeks
     the stars from which he came.
One day he will return to plant seed and cultivate his own bend.

Word to Smoke

For two days now, I have wanted to call you.
To tell you he is going to be fine.
I go to the phone and then remember.
A year and two months since you've been gone.

The cancer came quickly when you left.
No time to grieve, no time to remember.
Four times under the knife
No time to grieve—only surrender.

Something in him fights to live,
To win the battle for his reasons alone.
The surgery was a success this morning
They hooked his internal plumbing back up.

Since you have been gone, he hasn't been himself
Distant from this world as if part of him went with you.
I try to care for him as you did; it's just not the same
He plays a waiting game now—a game of high stakes.

In the next breath he says he has more to do here—
He can not or will not tell us what.
Thirsting after his own mystery
Like the man who knowing, does not know.

I write this down so we both can know.
To some region of ether, I send my angel, my word,
Match to paper, paper to ash, word to smoke.
My will is intention, so we both will know.

The Blessing

You left your father's house when you were still a child, golden
    and true.

You did not yet have his Blessing—he did not yet know how
    to give.

Wandering the world through long nights, your eyes upon a
    certain star,

Longing to close the great distance,

The Black Hole in your Soul sucking at every sweet fruit and
    bitter cup,

Learning the way of the Street and the way of the King's Court,

Making your way between the poles knowing them both.

Then a day or decade or an aeon passed, and growing tired of
    wandering—

You returned to your father's house alone and bent with a
    trace of wisdom—

A gift to him which you offered, the man you had become.

Then came the Blessing in silent breathing in the last days
    spent with him.

Passed along from body to body without word or deed.

What will you do now with this great gift, this fleshy burden,
    this Blessing?

Look at your sons, silhouetted against the horizon, trying to
    close the distance.

Personal / Interior

With the Moon

Today, I begin with the moon!
In waning, light—ever so slowly becomes darkness.
I let go of things known—certainties, illusions, and my
      dragons awaken.

The moon has long known its course, guided by the hand
      of mystery.
The soul too has its daemon, coming in the space between worlds,
Correcting a wandering course.

I left my home many moons ago while just a young lad.
Full of innocence and naiveté, a fool's faith—to this day yet intact.
The fool knows the way home while the wise one follows.

In the midst of this simple complexity,
The lady of my dreams says she will stay.
I am on the killing floor and she is my benevolent witness

I seek a place to fall apart where a new foundation can be built,
On the bedrock of my soul
Where faith and reason will have their marriage.

And the children of this marriage will know the secret course
      of the moon,
The fool will become wise and the wise one will follow no more.
The daemon will go home and the soul will be free to wander

Keepsake

On the night before the last day of the first grade.
My son said he wanted to give his teacher a gift,
A keepsake for her to remember him by.

He chose a uniform shirt from his soccer team
An item cherished by his mother and me—
A keepsake for us to remember him by.

"Your mother wouldn't want you to give it away," I told him.
"But I have two," he said and then—another keepsake:
"If you have two good shirts," he said, "It's best to give one away."

Middle of the Bridge

The middle-aged man no longer runs with wild things.
His life has changed for the better—so everyone says.
He got a steady job, entered the human race
And slowly his soul began to die.
He no longer sees the poetry in the fleeting moments of
Life or the flash of brilliance that lights his spirit with each sunrise
He wishes he could return to that earlier day when he lived carefree.

He is filled with grief, sadness darkens his day,
Sometimes exploding into anger.
The anger serves him well—or so he says.

He stands alone in the middle of the bridge of his life
And he is filled with a sense of awe at the mystery
And the paradox of it all.
He looks at his past and sees many things left undone,
And he understands grace.
He looks forward to the end of his days
And he understands hope.

He knows he will somehow make peace with himself.
He will see again the poetry in each fleeting moment and
The flash of brilliance that lights his spirit with each sunrise.

The Seeker

When I was still just a child,
I became a seeker of light—
In dark places—struggling with angels
And demons in the soul's midnight.

My father did not understand me
For I stepped into places he would not go.
"There are hills, mountains, and valleys" he said.
He knew very little of the pits that I cherished where wild
      things grow.

And now I've climbed up from these depths,
My eyes yet filled with shadow
Of death and dying to my best illusions—
I wait here for the night.

For now I am a man—and—
A seeker of shadow I have become.
In the light of day—I struggle with demons—
And angels in the soul's morning.

The Master

The Master called to me today. I heard his voice echoing as I looked into the mirror. The image I saw there, naked, pitiful, screaming out for love—love that was frozen in another time.

The Master lives in the wet miasma at the bottom of a spiraling path. It is there I must go. The path is made of broken dreams and reflections from the shattered mirrors of yesterday. I am tortured by these dreams and blinded by these reflections as I descend into this chaos.

At the bottom of the path amid all the images of my nightmares stands the Master like a guardian of the darkest midnight. He is not alone.

Stumbling blindly through my fear, driven by some greater need and led by a Grace I do not understand, I fall in abandon at the Masters feet. I am called to embrace this ominous figure of the night.

As I wrap myself in his shadow, my eyes are opened and I see who is with him—A child, and as I receive this child to myself, the love that was frozen in another time is rekindled in my heart. The sun dawns in this dark place and I see the Master become a humble servant

Discontent

Tangled, twisted, turning to and fro;
Like earthworms just uncovered—
This night, I cannot wrestle my dreams to sleep.

Searching for a place to rest that only the soul knows,
She knows—the soul knows.
Being still like some lizard on the mailbox by the front door—
He holds the key—changing colors to blend in—to survive.

I too go through my day changing hats for each part I play.
Then, in the end, discontentment comes like some house pet
Who's been left outside scratching at the door?

I touched the Grail once—it moved, shifted—
I began growing old.
Will I ever be content?

Scapegoat

When I was just a boy—almost young—
I was taken to a desert place.
It was a place of sacrifice,
And when the family spoke,
I knew I had to go—
For the family's sake, I had to go.

The desert was vast there, beautiful, forbidden
So I stepped across the line and I never looked back.

Many days or years or eons passed and I
Have learned to swim in these desert waters.
But now I am growing tired and I long to return
To the land of my father—
Washed clean of his sorrow.

Instructions

You can live by lies:
>   Laws you did not choose for yourself,
>   Follow leaders up ladders to the attic,
>   Busy yourself with memories of simpler days—
>   Or forget the past, look forward to some
>   Bright future when you can—
>   Live by the light of a hand me down truth;
>   Dismiss uncertainty to your basement;
>   Worship comfort, pleasure, pain, sorrow—
>   Suck at every breast that bares itself;

>   And, Or—

Take the down-turn:
>   Understanding from standing under—
>   Below bellies of crawling creatures;
>   In dark caves, mine for gold that was
>   Left by ancients only to find it rusting—
>   Until your soul cries out for rest—
>   Spend your nights weeping—all of your tears
>   Till your eyes bleed from the middle
>   And in your emptiness—find rest.

>   But then

You must return—
>   To your basement, pick up your uncertainty,
>   Go to your attic, burn all your souvenirs—
>   And trusting whatever you will,
>   Find your way to the forest where
>   The beasts will all know you,
>   And God will call you by your real name—

>   And then, who knows?

Visitor, Thief

Oh Love!
    Benevolent Visitor:

Who comes to my door, enters my house welcome,
Beckons me to travel, lifts the spirit high above ant hills
Beyond nests of eagles, clouds, stars, moons, in among heavens
Where Grace lives close to the veil of the Mystery.

Oh Love!
    Terrible Thief:

Who comes to my door, enters my house unbidden,
Robs the soul of its illusion of safety, takes me down, down, down,
Below shadowed streets, dark taverns, lost caves, in among Hades,
Where Hope falls broken upon rocks of despair.

I have followed your saints and dwelt with your sinners—
I have climbed your mountains and hid in your caves.
I have served in your temples and fallen drunk in your streets.
I have traveled your highways as Master and Slave.
And I am still here, still innocent, still free.

Oh Love!

To ride again upon your winds of change;
To dance again with your sons and daughters;
To soar without care above the tears of your children;
In among stars and moons and heavens to no end.

Or to be thrown down again in the mud at your feet,
And to know the fate of those whom you call.
To sweep the dust of the day out the door,
Only to find it again in the morn.

Oh Love!

Is there one among us who would follow your lead?
Is there anyone here who can contain your breath?

I am here torn to shreds, empty of all save the longing for you.
I await your knock upon my door.
No longer do I seek you, Oh Awful, Wonderful One.
I will wait here bent but not broken till the ends of the earth—
For your entry into my house, Oh Benevolent Visitor, Oh
Terrible Thief.

The Quiet

There is a quiet that comes in the midst of all busy-ness
Like gentle rainfall that's longing for your listening
Or some remote highway that's waiting for your wandering.

Going somewhere—not intent on getting there—
No longer searching, expecting to find—
Like children seeking the golden egg on Easter,
Or waiting for some happening like teenagers
In the mall parking lot on Friday night.

The butterfly that God painted,
Seeing that I have no net
Has landed on my shoulder.

ABOUT THE AUTHOR

Wayland Matthew Fox is a native Texan, married, with 9 children (Blend) 9 grandchildren (Blend), 2 great grandchildren and a huge extended family of friends and loved ones across the US. At present he is an independent contractor as a sales agent for a large company. He has spent much of the last 30 years exploring and speaking out about the issues and ramifications of alcoholism, abuse, and addiction.

He is the author of a non fiction book entitled First in the Mind and Heart which chronicles a great personal tragedy and the ensuing victory of life won through faith and determination.

He is active in the Mankind Project and his poetry largely stems from his own personal/spiritual work in what has been termed the mytho-poetic journey of the sacred masculine.

Currently living on Lake Livingston, he stays in touch with childhood friends, loves fishing, gardening, writing poetry, tinkering in his garage, a good argument and wants to live forever.